The Brownie Guide Law:
A Brownie Guide thinks of others before herself and does a Good Turn every day.

My Six is:

Contents

Enjoy all these great stories, games and activities!

6 — You decide!
Decision-making activities for you and your unit

8 — Super Brownie and the holiday challenge
Will Tahlia find the courage to climb?

12 — What sort of Brownie are you?
Which activities are your favourites?

14 — 'A world full of beauties and wonders'
Work towards a badge while you explore the beauty of the natural world

16 — Who's in your Six?
Do you know these Brownies? Are you one of them?

18 — Make magic layer squares and go bananas for banana bread!
Try these two recipes for some scrumptious snacks

20 — Bee prepared
Can Bella save her hive?

24 — How well do you know your Brownie Buddy?
Find out some secrets and surprises

26 — Jolly jokes and baffling brain-teasers
Can you stop laughing long enough to give all of these a try?

28 — Time-travelling Brownies
Use your imagination to move backwards and forwards through time

30 — Get snap happy!
Top tips for great photos

32 — Return of the Good Turn
Do something nice for someone

34 — Plarnations!
These flowers will never fade

36 — Brownies take charge!
Brownies tackle the First aid badge

38 — Dear Diary...
Six Brownies have a wild adventure

40 — The big Brownie quiz
Test your knowledge with these questions

42 — Hey there, Green Fingers!
Put a little more colour into the world

44 — Fantastic beasts around us
Animals have an amazing history

46 — Top secret adventure tent
Fancy having your own hide-away?

Front and back cover illustrated by Cathi Mingus

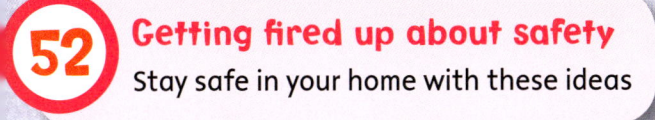

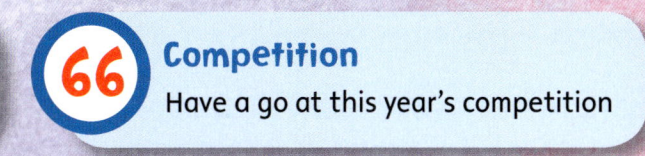

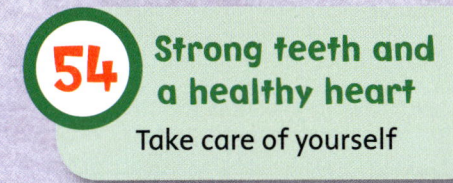

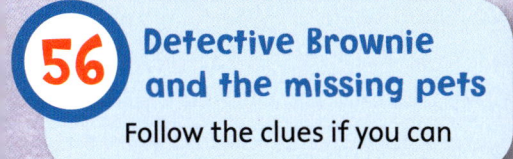

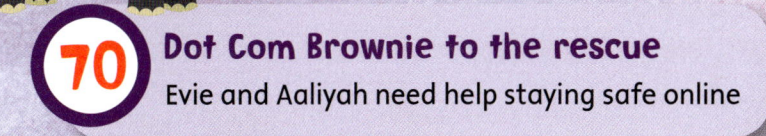

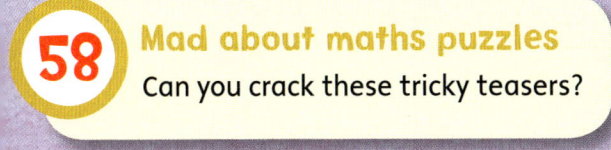

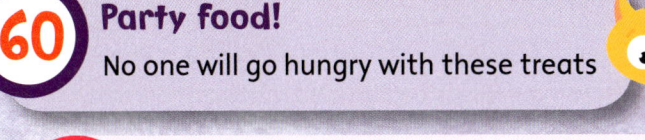

48	**Brownies – What's next?** Discover what Guides is all about	**64**	**Mexican hot chocolate party** New ways to enjoy this old favourite
52	**Getting fired up about safety** Stay safe in your home with these ideas	**66**	**Competition** Have a go at this year's competition
54	**Strong teeth and a healthy heart** Take care of yourself	**68**	**The power of air!** Try these experiments and you won't believe your eyes
56	**Detective Brownie and the missing pets** Follow the clues if you can	**70**	**Dot Com Brownie to the rescue** Evie and Aaliyah need help staying safe online
58	**Mad about maths puzzles** Can you crack these tricky teasers?	**74**	**Word puzzles** Can you get to the bottom of these?
60	**Party food!** No one will go hungry with these treats	**76**	**Puzzle and quiz answers** No peeking before you've finished them!
62	**Surprising facts about Brownies** Impress your friends and family		

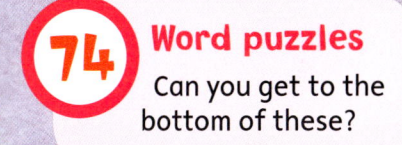

Be safe
You should be able to have a go at everything in your *Brownie Annual*, but sometimes it is a good idea to get some help. When you see this symbol, ask an adult if they can lend a hand.

Badges!
Look out for this sign. If you enjoyed the activity on that page, you might like to try the badge, too!

Web safe
This symbol means you should follow your Brownie Web Safe Code. To remember it, look up page 8 in your *Brownie Badge Book* or visit www.girlguiding.org.uk/brownies/websafe

Girlguiding UK
girls in the lead

Published by Girlguiding UK
17–19 Buckingham Palace Road
London SW1W 0PT
www.girlguiding.org.uk

© The Guide Association 2012

Girlguiding UK is an operating name of the Guide Association. Registered charity number 306016. Incorporated by Royal Charter.
ISBN 978 0 85260 2546

Girlguiding UK Trading Service ordering code 6005.

All Brownie and Guide photographs © The Guide Association.

Girlguiding UK would like to thank Sandra Bethray, Royal Russell School, 5th Croydon Brownies, 10th South Croydon Guides, the Sanderstead Rangers and their Leaders for their part in the development and production of this publication.

Project Editor: Margaret Swinson
Writers: Paul Darigan, Jenny Giangrande, Alison Griffiths, Donna Houghton, Abi Howson, Mariano Kälfors, Helen Mortimer, Catherine Murray, Karen Stapley, Margaret Swinson, Helen Thomas

Cover Design: Kim Haddrell
Designers: Angie Daniel, Helen Davis, Yuan Zhuang

Production: Wendy Reynolds
Project Coordinator: Helen Channa
Additional photographs: Frank Lane Picture Agency and Laura Ashman. Other photographs courtesy of Shutterstock unless otherwise stated.

Printed by Scotprint.

Readers are reminded that during the lifespan of this publication there may be changes to Girlguiding UK's policy, or legal requirements, that may affect the accuracy of the information contained within these pages.

MIX
Paper from responsible sources
FSC® C020007

You decide!

Here are two activties to help you and your Brownie friends make decisions together – and have fun.

WHAT TO DO

The perfect bedroom

You can do this activity with the rest of your Six or with some friends who aren't at Brownies. Tell them how much fun you have at Brownies. Maybe they will want to come along to see for themselves!

YOU WILL NEED
* scissors
* glue
* paper
* a catalogue of furniture and decorations

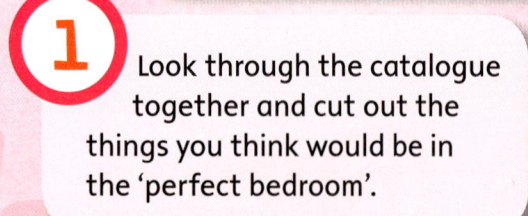

1 Look through the catalogue together and cut out the things you think would be in the 'perfect bedroom'.

2 Decide how the room will look and glue the pictures on to the paper.

3 Do the mini questionnaire below to find out if you are Superstar Decision Makers.

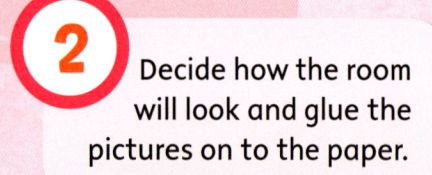

Mini questionnaire

1. Are you all happy with what is in the room?
2. Did everyone get a chance to have their say?
3. Did you decide what was going into the room in a fair way (did you vote or all take turns)?
4. Did you all have fun?

Results

If you answered all four questions with 'Yes' – congratulations, you are Superstar Decision Makers! Your Six or group can work together really well.

If you answered 'Yes' to two or three questions then you are Star Decision Makers! It's really important to let everyone in a group speak and for everyone to listen to their opinions. Keep practising and you'll be Superstar Decision Makers in no time!

If you answered 'Yes' to one or no questions, you might want to do some more activities to practise deciding together. Find a fair way to make decisions – you could vote on things that you don't all agree on.

If you'd like to practise working together in your Six, do this activity again but decide on a 'perfect holiday' using travel brochures. Cut out pictures of where you'd want to go and make a list of what you'd like to do.

Vote for your choice in surprising new ways...

WHAT TO DO

Funny votes

Leaders often ask Brownies to make decisions about the activities they could do as a unit or Six. Here's how to do that in a really funny way. These voting methods work whether you are with your whole unit or just making a decision in your Six.

Animal

This might get a bit noisy! Give each option an animal noise – like barking, meowing, roaring or mooing. Now voice a vote for your option using your animal noise.

Get active

This is good if you are feeling energetic! Give each option an action like star jumps, running on the spot, crouching down or hands on your head. Vote for your option by doing that activity.

Funny face

This is good if you don't have much space. Give each option a different expression – happy face, sad face, crying face or giggly face. If there are lots of Brownies present, you might want to make a rule that all of the same faces stand together so the Leader or Sixer can count easily.

BADGE LINK
Communicator

TAKE IT FURTHER

Why not think of new ways of voting and try them out?

Super Brownie and the holiday challenge

At the Brownie meeting

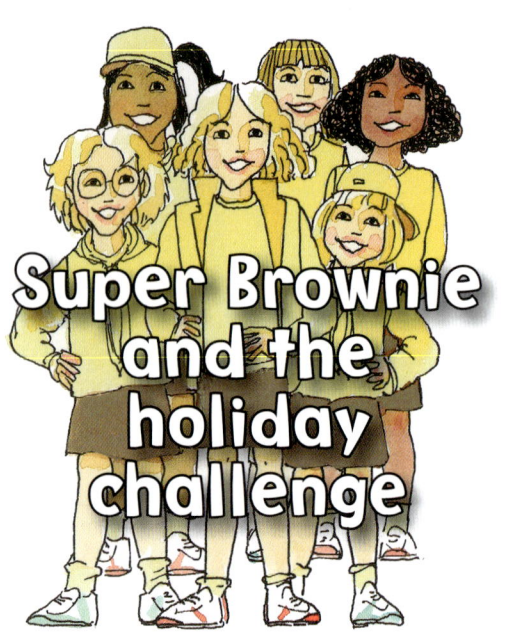

Good news – we're going to plan a Brownie Holiday. We'll get to camp outside!

Yeeeah! Yippee! Woohoo!

We need to raise some funds for new camping equipment. We need pans for hot chocolate, too. How could we do that, Brownies?

Sponsored silence.

Bag packing.

Baking cakes.

Selling jam.

Walking dogs.

We could do something SUPER ADVENTUROUS like a sponsored wall climb.

YES!

At the climbing centre…

Here's the rope.

Let's go.

Have you all got your helmets on?

Illustrated by Toni Goffe

8

(Sniff…)

What's wrong, Tahlia?

I'm scared! I don't think I'm brave enough.

Let's ask Super Brownie for some help.

I'm passing some Brownie courage around the circle.

At the supermarket…

WOOHOO!

Go Tahlia!

We're raising money for Brownie camp. Would you like to help?

We need some new tents and equipment.

Tahlia, would you like to read out how much we raised for our sponsored climbing?

£550!

Brilliant!

Even better news – we raised more than we needed so we have a bit left over for something special.

It's good we raised so much money.

What can we do with the extra money?

Super Brownie has a brainwave.

Let's plan a community event!

Six weeks later...

BIG BROWNIE BASH!

Where do you want to go first? There's so much to do.

I can't wait for the Brownie Bash!

10

Let's learn photography skills.
PHOTO WORKSHOP
How about a new sport like goalball? Everyone is blindfolded and they try to score a goal with a ball that has a bell inside.
Let's show our friends from school how much fun Brownies is.
See what the Brownie Adventure is all about!
Who's hungry? Everything looks delicious.
TRY SOME INTERNATIONAL FOODS
COME AND FIND OUT ALL ABOUT THE BROWNIES!
We'll have loads more Brownie friends before we know it!

What sort of Brownie are you?

Work your way through this chart with some of your friends who aren't Brownies. Start at the top and follow the arrows to discover each person's favourite type of activities and her ideal Brownie badge!

Inside or outdoors?

In

Behind the scenes or in the spotlight?

Behind — Spotlight

Learning or making? — **Speaking or singing?**

Learning — Making — Speaking — Singing

World cultures

Cooking or playing? — *Speaker* — *Entertainer*

Cooking — Playing

Cook — *Toymaker*

12

Out

Wet or dry?

Wet   Dry

Wet or really wet?   Scary ghost stories or sunny garden?

Wet   Really wet   Ghost stories   Garden

The badges

World cultures – Find out about traditions, food and costumes from around the world. See page 64.
Cook – Everyone loves having a friend who can make fairy cakes! See page 18.
Toymaker – Would you like to make a tricky jigsaw or a funny puppet? See page 34.
Entertainer – Use your skills to put on a show! See page 26.
Speaker – Got something to say? This sounds like the badge for you. See page 36.
Gardener – Try your green fingers at getting something to grow. See page 42.
Camper – Find out what it's like in the great outdoors. See page 46.
Watersports – There's lots of fun to be had on the water – try something new! See page 38.
Swimmer – Take to the water and swim like a fish. See page 38.

How many of these badges would you like to try? Which was the most popular among your friends? Do any of them want to go with you to the next Brownie meeting?

'A world full of beauties and wonders'

Here are some easy ways you can explore the world around you and one part of the Brownie Promise, 'To love my God'. You can even try these activities while you work towards earning a badge.

Brownie camper and Brownie camper advanced

Explore the great outdoors with a walk in the woods. Write down what you see and do in your diary. Make some time when you can sit quietly and think about the peaceful, open space around you?

Discovering faith

How often do you go to a place where you can learn about a faith? Is there singing? Reading from a book? Talking about beliefs? How do you feel when you listen to those words? Find out more about something that interests you and ask someone else what they think about it, too.

Environment

Did you know that no two snowflakes are the same? And no two Brownies are the same either! Ask your Brownie Buddy to go on a walk with you. Compare things like leaves, stones and flowers and talk about how they look the same but are different.

Stargazer

We can feel very small when we look up at the stars. Their light comes to us from many, many miles away. Do you know any stories about the stars or how they came to be?

Gardener

Some people like to think of their God as a great gardener who looks after all the living things on the Earth. A good gardener looks after plants, giving them what they need and protecting them from the wind and rain. Think about how every plant sprouts from a tiny seed and how the seed needs sunlight and water to grow. How can we care for the green things around us?

Seasons

Change is all around us. We notice it most in the different seasons. Which season is your favourite? Are there any cultural or religious festivals during that time? Do they relate to the season in any way?

Writer

Many religions have books with special writing about God, such as the Bible, the Talmud, the Koran and the Vedas. These books are hundreds or even thousands of years old! Do you have a favourite prayer, chant or piece of writing? Why not try to write your own?

Friend to animals

Go outside and count how many kinds of birds you can see or hear. Each one has its own special colours and song. Are any of them endangered? How does it affect us when animals are in danger?

Who's in your Six?

Do you recognise these characters from your Six? Which one are you? Write the names of Brownies you know next to each description if they fit.

In the Spotlight Brownie

A performer by nature, she loves singing, making up dances, dressing up in costume and performing plays – and she always has a smile on her face.

Names:

Adventure Brownie

She's a blur of activity and never sits still. You'll find her outdoors exploring, improving her time on the obstacle course or taking on the world at your unit's mini-Games.

Names:

Creative Brownie

It might be painting, photography or pottery – she is always making something! She might even dabble in origami, scrap-booking, baking or filmmaking.

Names:

Illustrated by Omar Aranda

Animal Lover Brownie

From hamsters to hippos, she's full of animal facts! It's her mission to make sure all pets are well looked after and protect wild animals that are in danger.

Names:

Science Investigator Brownie

Whether it's growing plants on her window ledge or gazing at the stars, this Brownie is fascinated by the world around her. She wants to know how everything works.

Names:

Bookworm Brownie

Her bag is full of books and her head is full of imaginary worlds. She's good at telling stories and is always the first to solve a word puzzle.

Names:

Magic layer squares

WHAT TO DO

This easy recipe doesn't need any mixing. It has six gooey, chewy layers and makes 16 5cm squares. Brownies with nut allergies can use oats for the chopped nuts and raisins instead of coconut.

INGREDIENTS

- 115g melted butter
- 150g digestive biscuit crumbs
- 90g flaked or shredded coconut
- 300g chocolate chips
- 100g chopped walnuts or pecans
- a 396g tin of condensed milk

1 Move a rack to the middle of the oven and preheat the oven to 180°C or gas mark 4.

2 Now add the layers in a 23cm x 23cm baking tray with a high rim in the order below.

Layer 1: Pour the melted butter into the tray.
Layer 2: Sprinkle the biscuit crumbs evenly over the butter.
Layer 3: Sprinkle the coconut on top of the crumbs.
Layer 4: Sprinkle the chocolate chips over the coconut.
Layer 5: Sprinkle the chopped nuts over the chocolate.
Layer 6: Drizzle the condensed milk evenly over the top.

Be safe

3 Bake for 30–35 minutes until a toothpick inserted into the middle of the tray comes out clean. Carefully remove the tray from the oven and let it cool on a wire rack.

4 Cut the mixture into 5cm squares and store them in the fridge.

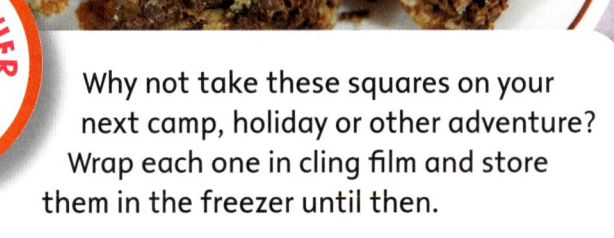

TAKE IT FURTHER

Why not take these squares on your next camp, holiday or other adventure? Wrap each one in cling film and store them in the freezer until then.

Go bananas for banana bread!

BADGE LINK — Cook

WHAT TO DO

This is more like cake than bread. Use up some bananas that are too squishy to eat.

INGREDIENTS

* butter for greasing
* 260g flour
* ¾tsp salt
* 1tbsp baking powder
* ¾tsp baking soda
* 70g chopped walnuts (optional)
* 3 large, very ripe bananas
* 1tsp lemon juice
* 3 eggs
* 80ml buttermilk
* 60ml vegetable oil
* 70g sugar

1 Preheat the oven to 175°C or gas mark 4 and grease a 23cm x 13cm loaf tin with butter.

2 Using a sieve, sift together the flour, salt, baking powder and baking soda and stir in the nuts (if using).

3 Peel the bananas and mash them with the lemon juice in another large bowl. Beat in the eggs one at a time, then the buttermilk, oil and sugar.

4 Mix the dry mixture into the wet mixture. Stir just enough to combine everything.

5 Pour the mixture into the tin. Bake for 60 minutes or until a toothpick inserted into the middle of the loaf comes out clean.

6 Cool the tin on a wire rack for 10 minutes before removing the banana bread. Slice and eat on its own or with cream cheese or butter.

Be safe

Bee prepared

Left, two, three, four, waggle waggle, *right* and – *crash*. Again. For the third time in a row I picked myself up, while Bella had another good laugh.

'Smooth moves, dancing queen!' she chuckled. 'You're getting much better – at falling over!'

Bella is my best friend. She's also a really great dancer. I'm not – and that's a problem. We're old enough to become Foragers, the bees who go out to find flowers and collect nectar. But we have to pass a test first, and the most important part of the test is the Waggle Dance. I just can't get the hang of it. Bella's helping me practise, but it's not going well.

'Come on, Brownie, try again. Take little steps so your legs don't get tangled up,' she suggested.

I got ready for another go, checking to make sure no one could see us. We weren't supposed to be dancing – we were on guard duty, keeping a look out for any danger. But the hive was busy and no one was watching us.

'OK, one, two and… Listen to that!' A loud angry drumming noise was coming from somewhere nearby. It stopped. Then it started again. And stopped. Then the drumming became louder than ever, and this time it kept going and going…

'It's Bess…' whispered Bella.

'And she's getting mad…' I replied.

'Let's go!' we shouted together, and zoomed off as fast as we could.

Let me explain. Bees of our age have two jobs: Guarding and Collecting. When the Foragers come back to the hive, they do a Tremble Dance – that's what makes the drumming noise. The Collectors hear the drumming, and run to meet them and help unload all the pollen and nectar they are carrying. It's a fun job because the Foragers tell you stories about what's going on outside the hive. Well, some of them do. Others – like Bess, for example – are always in a bad mood. If she doesn't get unloaded quickly she gets very angry. And this time, it seemed that no Collectors were around. Although we were on Guard duty, we'd have to help.

Illustrated by Alexandra Ball

We raced up to Bess and skidded to a stop.

'We're here!' I gasped. She was making so much noise she didn't hear, so I had to shout it again: 'WE'RE HERE!'

Bess stopped her Tremble Dance, but she was still shaking with fury. 'Where have you been, you useless grubs?'

'Sorry!' squeaked Bella, bravely. 'We're not meant to be Collecting – we're Guards today.'

'Don't give me excuses!' roared Bess. 'Get unloading, now!'

But even though she was shouting at the top of her voice, we could hardly hear Bess. Cries and yells, crashes, bangs and furious buzzing had all erupted from somewhere close by. It sounded horribly like…

'A raid!' A messenger almost knocked us down as she streaked past. 'The wasps are here! A raid! All bees to the south store!'

Bella and I gasped in horror. We had been guarding the south store! The wasps must have been spying, and as soon as they saw us fly away to Bess, they had attacked! We were going to be in trouble.

When we made it to the south store, the scene was dreadful. Cracked and broken honeycombs scattered the floor. Injured bees were being helped away. Oozing trails of spilled honey led from the door to a huge hole in the wall, where the wasps had escaped with an enormous store of honey.

Bernice, our team leader, spotted Bella and me as we gazed around.

'There you are! I'm so glad you're OK. What happened?'

She was really worried, but as we began to tell our story, that soon changed.

'You left your guard post?' she shouted. 'What were you thinking? You two left this store wide open and now the wasps have stolen all this honey and hurt our bees – and it's all your fault!'

A bee with a hurt leg limped past. Bella began to sniffle.

'We're sorry. We were just trying to help Bess.'

'That's no excuse! You do not leave your guard post for any reason. Well, if you two aren't responsible enough to be Guards, maybe you can manage some cleaning. I want this storeroom clean and tidy by the end of the day. Get scrubbing!'

21

I was shocked. Cleaning is a baby job, done by bees who are too young to take their Guard and Collector tests. I couldn't believe Bernice was making us join the babies. I knew we should not have left our Guard posts, but we had only been trying to help.

We spent the rest of the day sweeping up smashed combs and mopping up pools of honey. At last there was only one corner left to clean. Some odd-looking red petals were scattered there.

'Hey Bella, what are these?'

We puzzled over the petals together. They looked like clover petals, but we had never seen any this colour. Clover was normally white or purple, not red.

The next day we were allowed to join the others for a Foraging lesson. Bernice led us all out of the hive and took us on a long flight to a meadow we hadn't visited before. She split us up into pairs and we all set off to look for good nectar.

Bella and I found a small patch of buttercups, but we didn't get much nectar from them. We flew on further, wanting to get lots and show Bernice what good, useful Foragers we were. But we had no luck.

'Should we turn back now?' asked Bella nervously. 'We're a long way from Bernice, we don't want to get into more trouble.'

'Just a bit further,' I said. 'Let's see what's over the hedge.'

So we buzzed off. I was determined to find some fantastic nectar. We zoomed up over the hedge. At first I couldn't see any flowers, but then I noticed an odd patch of something red on the ground, a long way across the field.

'Bella, look over there!'

'What? Oh, that red stuff? What is it?'

'It's the same colour as those petals we found in the south store yesterday! Let's go and see!'

Without another word we shot off. By now we were miles away from the others, but we had to know for sure. As we got closer, we slowed down and dropped to the ground. We crawled the last little way till we could see the flowers clearly.

'Look at that! Red clover! I've never seen that anywhere before.'

'The wasps must have dropped those petals when they raided our hive. Do you think their hideout is somewhere nearby?'

'It must be!' I whispered. 'Come on. If we can find it we'll know where the wasps live. Then we can look out for any more surprise attacks.'

Slowly, silently, we crept forwards. A low droning sound grew louder and shadows began to flit over our heads: guard wasps, looking for spies.

'Stay here,' I whispered to Bella. 'I'll go on.'

Looking round, I spotted a fallen poppy petal. I dragged it over my head and crawled forward. Hidden underneath the petal and moving slowly, I could creep right into the wasps' territory.

Finally, I saw a hole in the earth with wasps buzzing in and out. Their hideout! I checked the sun to find out exactly where I was. Then, heart thumping, I crept back to Bella.

'Let's get out of here!' I hissed. We flew out of there so fast, my wings were shaking when we finally reached Bernice and the others.

'So you're finally back. And where's your nectar? You don't seem to have any at all.'

Panting, we told our story as fast as we could.

'Well done you two!' exclaimed Bernice. 'OK, so where is the wasps' hideout?'

This was the real test. Bees don't point and say 'Over there!' – we do the Waggle Dance instead. All the steps and turns in the dance are a secret code that tells other bees where to find something. So now I had to do the dance to tell everyone where the wasps were coming from. If I messed it up, they wouldn't be able to find it.

I took a deep breath and stepped out: one, two, left turn, waggle waggle… right through to the end. It was perfect! For the first time ever I didn't fall over my own feet, crash into someone or announce that nectar was located on the moon. I did it!

At once, Bernice sent the fastest bees back to our hive to warn the others. We followed, and on the way we passed several bees heading back the way we had come.

'Spies heading out to the wasps' nest,' whispered Bernice. 'They will warn us next time the wasps set out on a raid.'

And they did. Later that morning we got an alert from the spies. The whole hive waited, quiet but ready. As soon as the wasps came in sight, we all shot out and surrounded them in a furious, buzzing golden swarm. The wasps were terrified and couldn't get away fast enough. They wouldn't be troubling us again.

'Well done, you two!' exclaimed Bernice when it was all over. 'You're both going to make great Foragers. In fact you have passed your test, and you can start your new work tomorrow!'

Bella and I high-fived.

'And… You are also going to get Queen's Bee awards for saving the hive. How about that?'

We were speechless. The Queen's Bee award is the highest honour any bee can earn. We'd get to meet the Queen and have a special feast. It was too good to be true! So why did Bella look worried?

'Come on,' she sighed. 'Let's go and practise curtseying – can't have you falling over in front of the Queen…'

23

How well do you know your Brownie Buddy?

Get to know a familiar friend even better with this quiz. Then let your Brownie Buddy quiz YOU!

1 My Brownie Buddy's favourite thing to do at meetings is:
a) be adventurous outside
b) make a clever craft
c) try something new and challenging
d) whatever everyone else wants to do.

2 When it comes to outdoor activities, my Brownie Buddy:
a) likes to stay inside where it's warm
b) runs into the rain while everyone else is putting on their coats
c) will give anything a try once but prefers sunny days
d) only wants to do the things she already likes.

3 Working on badges is:
a) something my Brownie Buddy loves. She wants them all!
b) fun but she doesn't feel like doing all of them
c) a lot of work. My Brownie Buddy prefers activities instead
d) a chance to try something new and she's not afraid of that!

4 If my Brownie Buddy were an animal she would be:
a) something fast like a cheetah
b) something colourful like a peacock
c) something funny like a monkey
d) something furry like a cat.

5 My Brownie Buddy is a good friend who has a talent for:
a) making people laugh
b) cheering others up
c) getting other Brownies to join in
d) helping whoever needs it.

6 When my Brownie Buddy grows up, the first thing she wants to do is:

a) travel round the world
b) find a really great job
c) have a family
d) go to university.

7 My Brownie Buddy is frightened of:

a) trying strange-looking foods
b) meeting new people
c) talking in front of a crowd
d) nothing!

8 My Brownie Buddy's best subject in school is:

a) art – she likes colour
b) maths – numbers are exciting
c) history – there's so much going on
d) science – whizz, bang, boom!

9 If I told my Brownie Buddy a joke that wasn't funny she would:

a) laugh anyway
b) tell me it was terrible
c) tell me a joke of her own
d) share the joke with someone else.

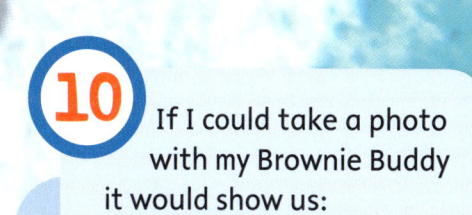

10 If I could take a photo with my Brownie Buddy it would show us:

a) climbing a very tall tree at an activity centre
b) covered in glitter doing a Brownie craft
c) eating biscuits at one of our meetings
d) making a tent to use as a secret hideout.

25

Jolly jokes and baffling brain-teasers

Boggle your friends with these brain-teasers and tangle them with these tongue twisters!

Jokes

How do skeletons talk to their mates? On a mobile bone! (Dreadful!)

How did the farmer fix his dungarees? With a cabbage patch of course! (Get it?)

I was reading a great book today – The History of Glue. I couldn't put it down. (Grooooaaaann!)

Why did the hedgehog cross the road? To see his flatmate. (Oooh! That's painful.)

Knock, knock!
Who's there?
Cows go.
Cows go who?
No! Cows go mooooo!

What do you get if you cross a centipede with a parrot? A walkie-talkie.

What has eight legs and ticks? A clocktopus. (Definitely NOT funny.)

Illustrated by John Shelley

What do mermaids eat for breakfast?
Mermalade on toast!

Tongue-twisters

How much dew does a dewdrop drop if dewdrops do drop dew? They do drop, they do. As do dewdrops drop if dewdrops do drop dew.

Red lolly, yellow lolly.

I scream, you scream, we all scream for ice cream!

Swan swam over the sea. Swim, swan, swim! Swan swam back again. Well swum swan!

A Tudor who tooted the flute tried to tutor two tooters to toot. Said the two to the tutor, 'Is it harder to toot or to tutor two tooters to toot?'

Brain-teasers

a) What can you keep after giving it to someone?

b) What goes round and round the wood but never into the wood?

c) I am a number. When you add me to another number it does not change. When you multiply me by another number, I do not change. Who am I?

d) When you say my name I break. What am I?

e) What can't you give away as it will always come back to you?

Answers on page 76.

Time-travelling Brownies

Lots of books and films have been written about time travel – the idea that you can go back into the past or forwards into the future. Unfortunately no one has built a time machine yet, but you can use your imagination and memory to do the hard work!

The Past – Words of wisdom

What is your earliest memory? Think about some things you used to find difficult or scary but now do all the time. Do you remember your first day at school or at Brownies? What would you say to your younger self when she was feeling scared? Write down three things to help her below:

The Present – Time capsule treasure

Draw a picture of yourself and add some words describing what you are like today. Don't forget to add the date. Look at your picture in a year's time. Will you be different from the picture? Will you describe yourself in the same way?

The Future – Brownies in space?

What will the world be like in 100 years' time? What badges might Brownies work towards – Astronaut? 3D-filmmaker? Draw your ideas.

Get snap happy!

A great photo makes you feel like you are in the action. Photographer David Hosking and his team have travelled all over the world for Frank Lane Picture Agency, snapping kangaroos in Australia, swans in Japan and lions in Tanzania. Here are David's top tips for amazing photos.

1 Get closer
Don't be afraid of getting close to your subject with a zoom lens – or just walk nearer if you can.

2 Don't delay
A great moment might last for only a second or two. Be prepared to press that button!

3 Keep it simple
The best pictures are often the simplest. Don't worry about getting everything into one photo.

4 Think about what is in the photo
The subject doesn't have to be in the middle of the picture. Try putting it on one side.

5 Be selective
Study the whole picture and then capture one detail in sharp focus. Other details may be a bit blurry. This is called 'depth of field'.

Frank Lane Picture Agency

6 Focus on your subject

There might be a lot going on in your picture. Make sure the subject is the most important thing!

BADGE LINK
Hobbies

7 Capture movement

Some action shots will turn out blurry because the subject is moving, but other shots capture a great moment where the subject is frozen in time. This might be birds in flight or a cat running. These photos take practice.

8 Make the light work for you

The best light of the day is sunrise and the second best is sunset. Use the shadows and colours to take amazing photos but don't be afraid to turn on the flash too.

9 Check the weather

Don't be defeated by the weather – even a rainy day might bring a rainbow!

10 Be bold

How can you take the best photo? Try lying on the ground, sneaking up to your subject and using your imagination. Try not to shake the camera when you take the picture.

31

Return of the Good Turn

There are Good Turns all around you just waiting to happen! Which of these activities will you do today?

Out and about

✶ Let someone else go first. Give up your seat on the bus to a person who needs it more than you do. Or hold a shop door open to let someone through instead of rushing through first.

✶ Help someone struggling with their bags. Can you see someone carrying lots of heavy shopping? What about someone trying to go up some stairs with a baby buggy or suitcase?

✶ Return something that is lost. If you spot someone dropping their gloves or a baby's toy falling out of their pushchair, let them know! Or if you can't, hand things in to a lost property office or police station.

✶ Help someone new. Do you remember what it's like to be new? Is there someone at Brownies or school who needs help finding their way around?

✶ Spend wisely. Could you donate pocket money to a charity? Buy a present for someone?

At home

* Clear up. Is your room always a mess? Do you clear your plate away after a meal? Try to leave places tidier than you found them by putting things away and putting rubbish in the recycling container or bin.

* Share! Even chocolate tastes better when someone else gets some too. You can also share a story, a joke, a toy, your time or even a song with your family.

* Lend something. Do you have a favourite book that your friend would like to borrow? If you both read it, you'll be able to talk about how good it is!

* Cheer up someone who is tired. Has Mum had a long day looking after your baby brother? Has Dad spent all afternoon running errands and buying groceries? Maybe your sister didn't do so well in her exam. Help them put their feet up so they can relax for a bit.

* Give someone a compliment. Everyone likes hearing something nice about themselves. Find three people to compliment today and you'll be spreading the smiles around!

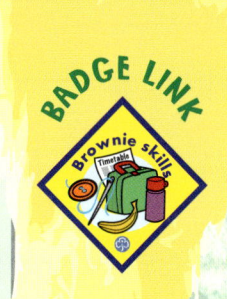

Plarnations!

Plastic bags take a very long time to break down and lots of animals die every year because they eat them. Plarn is the 'wool' made from plastic bags. Have a go at making a 'plarnation' to see how many you can recycle, and make the world a more beautiful place at the same time.

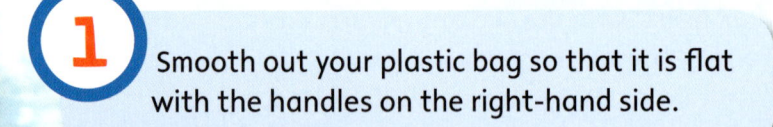

1 Smooth out your plastic bag so that it is flat with the handles on the right-hand side.

2 Fold it in half lengthways so that the two handles come together.

YOU WILL NEED
- several plastic shopping bags
- scissors
- pipe cleaner

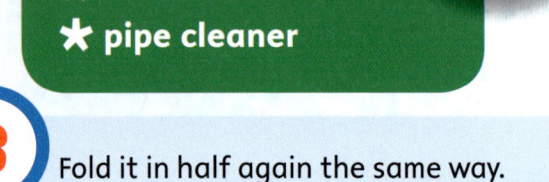

3 Fold it in half again the same way. You should now have a long, thin strip.

4 Chop off the handles and a narrow strip from the bottom of the bag.

5 Cut the remaining strip lengthwise in 2cm-wide portions. When you unfold all of these, they should make long, thin loops of plastic bag.

6 Make your bags into plarn. For each carnation, you need 20–30 loops.

7 Gather the loops together and hold them in the middle.

8 Now fold the top half down and the bottom half up so that the loops are in a concertina. There should be three layers.

9 Wrap the pipe cleaner tightly around the middle of the concertina, leaving a length of pipe cleaner to be the stem.

10 Cut through the ends of the loops in the concertina, and fluff out the plarnation.

11 Try making plarnations with different-coloured bags.

BADGE LINK
Craft
Environment

35

Brownies take charge!

'Did you enjoy that?' asked Lucy, the doctor who'd come in specially to help 2nd Dington Brownies with their First aid badge.

'YES!' chorused the Brownies as they sat cross-legged in their Pow-wow circle, clutching their new badges.

'That's great,' said Lucy. 'Now if someone's been injured or isn't well, you'll know how to help them.' The Brownies smiled and felt pleased at this – except Mia, a younger Brownie, who had a worried look on her face.

'Are you all right, Mia?' asked Sam, the Brownie Leader. 'Didn't you like first aid?'

'I thought it was great,' Mia answered. 'I was just thinking that we can't all be everywhere. What if someone has an accident and there isn't a Brownie there to help?'

'Hmmm, you have a point there,' said Sam.

Lucy nodded and said, 'If everyone in our community knew first aid, I think we'd all be much safer.'

'What do the rest of you think?' asked Sam.

Lots of Brownies in the circle threw their hands up to speak – they all had something to say.

'Yes, Chloe?' asked Sam. Chloe's face was turning purple, she wanted to speak so badly!

'I think so too!' Chloe burst out. 'When I broke my arm falling off my rollerblades even my Mum wasn't sure what to do – except to take me to A&E.'

'Kate, what do you think?' Sam asked a new Brownie who had her hand up shyly.

'I'd be scared if I had collapsed and no one knew how to help me,' said Kate quietly.

'What about you, Helena?' said Sam.

Helena took a deep breath and said, 'I thought the first aid stuff about blood was really gross but I still think everyone should know how to stop bleeding. They could save someone's life.'

'Well then,' said Sam, looking round at everyone, 'how could we help people in Dington to learn more about first aid?'

The Brownies looked at each other, unsure. Mia started whispering to Chloe, who was sitting next to her.

'Chloe and Mia?' said Sam. 'Pow-wows are for sharing ideas all together, not just in pairs. Can you tell everyone what you're talking about?'

'Sorry,' said Mia. 'I just wasn't sure if it was a silly idea.'

Illustrated by Omar Aranda

'There's no such thing as a silly idea!' said Sam encouragingly.

'OK, well… we thought maybe we could get people to come to a meeting at the community centre and maybe Lucy could teach them first aid?' suggested Mia.

Lucy the doctor put both thumbs up – she thought it was a great idea.

Chrissy had her hand up to reply. 'Yeah, and we could help teach them too!'

Roohi was next to offer an idea. 'And we could give them a First aid badge at the end!'

Everyone giggled and nodded.

'Let's make posters to get people to come,' suggested Gemma.

'We could raise money for Brownies at the same time,' Yasmin said. Everyone started chatting excitedly. Sam put up her hand for silence and everyone fell quiet again.

'These are fantastic ideas,' said Sam. 'Let's hold a vote. Close your eyes and put your hand up if you're in favour of holding a First aid badge event for the people of Dington.' Every Brownie's hand shot up. 'You can open your eyes now, Brownies. It's agreed – we'll do it!'

It took a few weeks of planning, organising and inviting but eventually the big day came. Adults and children from all over Dington filled the community centre. The Brownies even asked the mayor to come!

The first aid evening was a huge success. The Brownies were on hand to give demonstrations of everything from broken bones to the recovery position. Everyone learned a lot and had fun. The 1st Dington Guides also helped out by selling food they'd made for their Cook badge.

At the end of the evening the mayor stood up to make a speech. 'Well done to everyone who has gained their First aid badge this evening!' The Brownies started clapping and everyone else joined in. 'I know I've learned a huge amount tonight and have made lots of new friends along the way. Thanks to the Brownie Leaders and to Lucy, but most of all to the Brownies who came up with this idea in their Pow-wow all by themselves. I can't wait to see what they'll come up with next. Girls can do anything – right Brownies?'

All together the Brownies replied: 'YES!'

Dear Diary...

The girls from 1st Anywhere Brownies have been to Foxlease Training and Activity Centre to try out some activities! As part of their Brownie camper badge they have been keeping camp diaries. Let's see what they thought...

In the Spotlight Brownie:

I love dressing up so I wasn't looking forward to a whole weekend in waterproofs and wellies. But then we got to learn circus skills like juggling and plate-spinning. They weren't easy but I was so proud when I managed to juggle with three balls. I'm going to be the star of our next talent show!

Adventure Brownie:

I've been waiting for this weekend for AGES. Everyone knows I'm good at running, climbing and swimming, and I was the first one up the stairs of the abseil tower. But when I got to the top it seemed really high and my legs went all wobbly. But with lots of encouragement from the other Brownies I made it down. Now I can't wait to go again!

Creative Brownie:

When we were told we had to make our own raft to get across the lake, we were all a bit nervous. But then I thought that the poles were just like giant lolly sticks and the barrels were like big cotton reels and it was lots of fun. We built our raft and made it across the lake in one piece.

Bookworm Brownie:

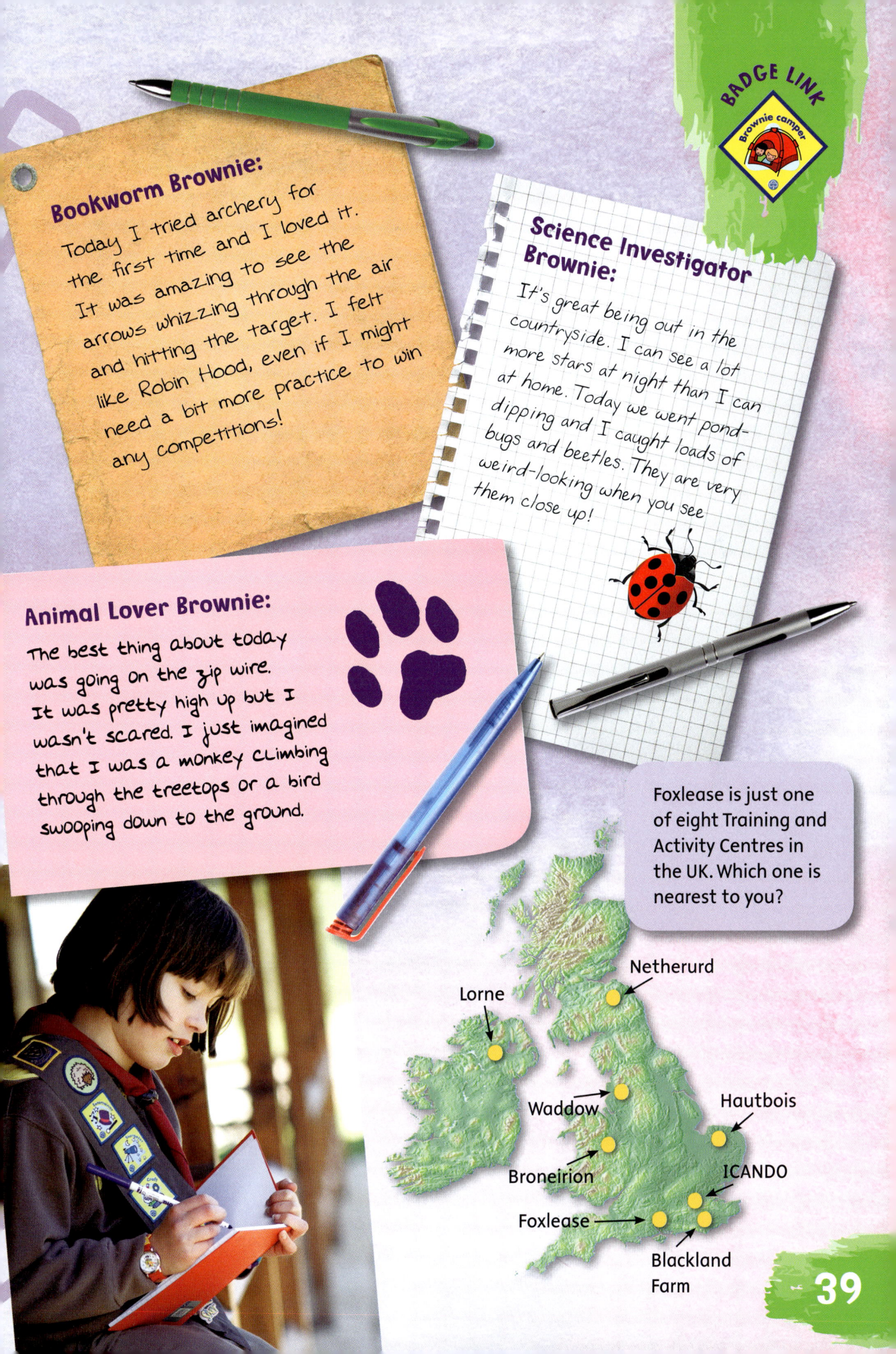

Today I tried archery for the first time and I loved it. It was amazing to see the arrows whizzing through the air and hitting the target. I felt like Robin Hood, even if I might need a bit more practice to win any competitions!

Science Investigator Brownie:

It's great being out in the countryside. I can see a lot more stars at night than I can at home. Today we went pond-dipping and I caught loads of bugs and beetles. They are very weird-looking when you see them close up!

Animal Lover Brownie:

The best thing about today was going on the zip wire. It was pretty high up but I wasn't scared. I just imagined that I was a monkey climbing through the treetops or a bird swooping down to the ground.

BADGE LINK
Brownie camper

Foxlease is just one of eight Training and Activity Centres in the UK. Which one is nearest to you?

- Netherurd
- Lorne
- Waddow
- Hautbois
- Broneirion
- ICANDO
- Foxlease
- Blackland Farm

39

The big Brownie quiz

Test your knowledge of Brownie history with these fun questions.

You can find the answers on page 76.

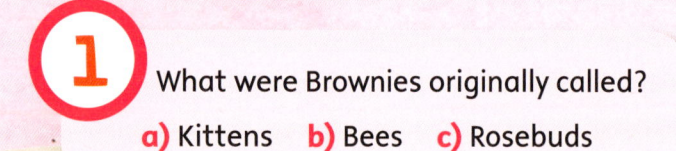

1 What were Brownies originally called?
a) Kittens   b) Bees   c) Rosebuds

2 True or false?
The Brownie story was taken from the book *The Brownies and Other Tales* by Juliana Horatia Ewing.

3 What age did you have to be to join Brownies until 1937?
a) 6   b) 8   c) 9

4 In which country are Brownies known as Bulbuls ('Bluebirds')?
a) India   b) France   c) Australia

5 Which of these have never been Brownie wear?
a) A yellow jumper and jogging trousers
b) A brown dress and yellow tie
c) A yellow tracksuit with a brown baseball cap

6 In 1975 Brownies greeted the delegates at the WAGGGS World Conference at Sussex University. Which flower did they give each delegate as a gift?

a) A red rose   b) A daisy   c) A pink fuchsia

7 Which of these titles was **not** the name of a test that Brownies could do until 1967?

a) The Golden Bar
b) The Golden Hand
c) The Golden Camel

8 Which of these has **not** been the name of a Brownie Six?

a) Gnome   b) Troll   c) Fairy

9 Which of these members of the Royal Family was not a Brownie?

a) The Queen
b) Princess Margaret
c) The Duchess of Cambridge

10 True or false?

In 2007 Brownies took part in a world record attempt for the largest sleepover at the BT Tower.

41

Hey there, Green Fingers!

Bee friendly

Trees and plants are great for cleaning the air. Why not plant one that will provide a home for birds, food for bees and butterflies, and something nice for everyone to look at? Examples include fruit trees, pussy willow, mountain ash, buddleia and chestnut. If you do not have a garden perhaps your local council will allow you to plant something in a nearby park. Bluebells, primroses and lavender smell wonderful and bees love them.

Feed me!

If you would like to start growing plants there is a very easy way to keep their soil full of nutrients – put in some compost. You will need a big compost bin with a lid at the top and an open end at the bottom that can rest on bare earth or grass. You can often get one from your local council. Put in a mixture of half 'green' items (vegetable peel, apple cores, tea bags, bread, coffee grounds) and half 'brown' items (torn up cereal packets, newspaper, egg boxes) from your usual kitchen waste. Do not put in meat products or cheese. In a year's time your bin will be full of crumbly black compost that plants will love. You can use it in many of the activities on these pages.

Illustrated by Alexandra Ball

Kitchen craft

If you like to cook, there are some herbs that will taste great in recipes as well as being bee-friendly. Why not plant a small herb garden with chives, sage, thyme, mint and rosemary? *The Brownie Cookbook* is full of tasty recipes you can try.

BADGE LINK
- Environment
- Friend to animals
- Gardener
- Wildlife explorer

Toad of Toad Hall

If you'd like to keep slugs away from your plants, make a toad hall by knocking a doorway 8cm wide and 4cm high in the top of a clay plant pot that is 20cm across. Place the pot upside down in a shady spot near some water. You can also turn a pot on its side and bury half of it in the soil. Put some leaves in the pot for the toad's bed. You can also make different houses for birds, bumblebees, hedgehogs, bats and ladybirds.

Be safe

43

Fantastic beasts around us

We share our home with some amazing animals. Find out more about them here.

Fabulous creatures

In prehistoric times Britain was home to woolly mammoths, brown bears and aurochs (giant cattle). Later on the grey wolf and great auk were hunted to extinction. Some animals have been brought back to Britain, such as the reindeer, beaver, eagle owl and wild boar. Think about how our lives would be different if the cave lion, woolly rhinoceros and lynx still lived here.

Come back home

See how you can provide a home for smaller animals on page 43. There are lots of other ways to care for the green spaces near you. Picking up litter is a great way to make the animals that live in a park safer. Why not organise a clean-up walk with your Brownie friends and Leader?

Illustrated by John Shelley

If it's up to me...

Put all the items you can into the recycling bin rather than throwing them away. If you like growing flowers, fruit and veg, try making compost (see page 42 for how) and keep a small bin in the kitchen for compost scraps.

Next time someone does the food shopping, make a list of all the plastic wrapping, cartons and boxes that come with each product. Are they all necessary? Could you make do with fewer or none of them? Send your list to a supermarket and encourage it to use less packaging.

BADGE LINK
Wildlife explorer

A familiar face

Many pets have been domesticated – that is, made friendlier and part of human society – from a wild ancestor. When you look at your cat, do you see a fierce tiger? Does your dog remind you of a grey wolf? Who would imagine that a pink pig is related to a shaggy boar with long tusks? Or that a pet parrot or lizard might have been born in a faraway jungle? What could your pet's story be?

45

Top secret adventure tent

Everyone likes to have a place they can go to be alone or have some special time with friends. Here are some ideas to build a hideout for yourself. What would be your favourite?

Washing line tent

Have you been on a Brownie camp? Think about what you liked about your tent. Could you hear birdsong in the morning? Catch a glimpse of the stars at night? Maybe it was being so close to nature but staying dry. Ask an adult to tie a washing line between two points in your garden. The line should be a bit higher than your head when you're sitting down. Drape a sheet over the string and pin the ends down with stones.

Table tent

Would you like to start a club with some Brownie buddies? Drape a sheet or blanket over a large table. Put some cushions under the table and you've got an easy-peasy meeting place for you and some friends.

Tunnel tent

A tunnel tent makes a good spot for you to spend some time alone. You can read or write in a journal, have a sneaky snack or do some colouring. Ask an adult to move a sofa away from the wall. Drape a sheet or blanket over the back of the sofa so it touches the floor behind the couch. Pull the ends away from the sofa to make a bit of room and secure them on the ground with something heavy. You've now got a secret tunnel all to yourself!

BADGE LINK
brownie camper

TAKE IT FURTHER

If you like doing things with tents, why not ask your Brownie Leader if you can visit a Training and Activity Centre (TAC) with your unit? There's lots to do there besides camp, which means there is fun for everyone! See pages 38-39.

47

Brownies – What's next?

1. Bye, Katie!

2. Where's your sister Katie going?
She goes to Guides.

3. What's Guides?
Guides is what comes after Brownies.

4 Later at the Brownie meeting…

We wanted to ask about Guides.

My sister goes and we know they wear blue tops.

I don't like blue. Brownie yellow is better!

What IS Guides?

5 I'll tell you four things but we'll have to ask the Guides to come and show us.

Yeah!!

'Guides is the next guiding section after Brownies.'

'Guides have amazing blue tops and other gear.'

'Guides have Patrols, Patrol Leaders and Patrol Seconds instead of Brownies' Sixes, Sixers and Seconds.'

'Guides have their own activities, challenges, Go For Its! and badges!'

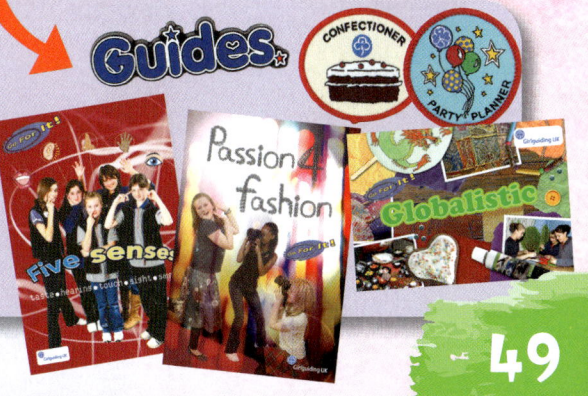

49

6 Later, the Guides come to Brownies...

They look bigger and older – I'm a bit nervous.

I hope the Guides are nice.

7

Hi Brownies!

Let's talk about what being a Guide is like.

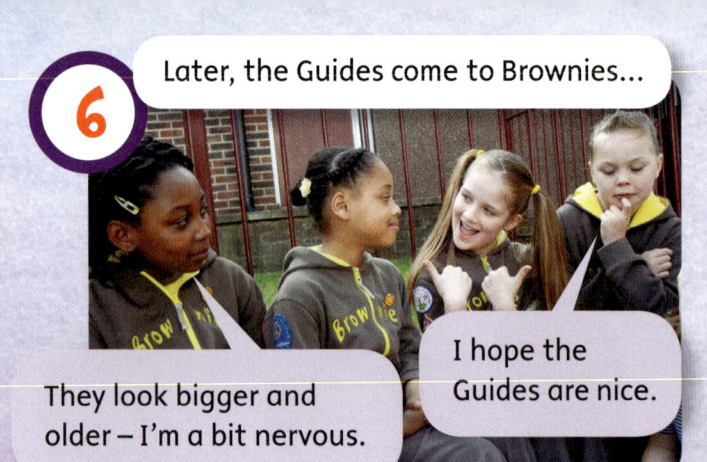

8 We have three activity areas for you to choose from in your Sixes. What do you want to do first?

9 The first area is 'Everything About Guides', the second is 'Meeting New Friends and Making Decisions' and the third is 'Adventures at Guides'.

10 At the 'Everything About Guides' area...

Do you want to try on some Guide wear?

I like the stripy shirt.

What are those?

This is my *G File*. It has everything about the guiding family, the Promise, the badges and Go For It! challenges.

50

11 At the 'Meeting New Friends and Making Decisions' area...

Hi, I'm Layla and this is Rebecca and Erin. We like choosing activities. Last summer we asked to have a water balloon fight and it was fun!

That's awesome! Last summer we decided to learn about pizza making. We got to visit an Italian restaurant and learn from a real chef.

12 At the 'Adventures at Guides' area...

Ready to go climbing?

I'm a bit scared but if you can do it, so can I!

13 We don't just go climbing for our adventures. Last October we went to the BIG GIG pop concert. There were thousands of Guides there!

It was such a good day!

14 So, what did you think of your meeting with the Guides?

We LOVED it.

They were really nice.

I can't wait till I'm ten so I can go to Guides.

Now I have lots of adventure ideas I want to do at Brownies before I go to Guides.

51

Getting fired up about safety

In Brownies you can work towards a fire safety badge. Here are some other ways to learn about staying safe in your home.

Stop, drop and roll

If your clothes catch fire you can put them out in three easy steps. If someone else's clothes are on fire, help them to do the three steps. You can also cover them with a blanket to help put the fire out.

1. Stop moving and stand still. You can't escape the fire by running from it.
2. Drop to the floor where the ground will cover part of you and smother the fire.
3. Roll back and forth, turning over and over so that the fire is put out.

Follow the signs

You will notice the fire by:

* a smoke detector alarm going off
* the smell or appearance of smoke in the house
* seeing a fire burning
* feeling a door that is too hot to open.

Put that fire out!

All homes should have a smoke detector. If you see a fire start, get an adult to put it out while it is still small. Do not stay in the room.

Let's talk about it

Discuss with everyone in your home what basic fire safety means for the following things:

* oven, hob, grill, microwave, toaster
* fireplaces and heaters
* cigarettes.

The danger of smoke

Smoke is as dangerous as fire. If you smell it, crawl on your hands and knees to avoid breathing it in. It may help to put a wet hanky over your nose and mouth. If you can't escape the room, put some rolled-up clothes or a towel against the crack under the door then try to escape from a window. If the window is too high to jump from, open it and shout and wave to attract attention.

Escape plan

Talk to your parents or carers about the best routes for escape. Look at all the windows and doors to see what exits may be possible and which ones could never be used, such as a very high window. Remember that the route you use will depend on the location of a fire. Practise your escape plan with everyone and agree on a meeting place outside.

Get out, get help

Alert everyone in the house by yelling 'FIRE!'. Do not take anything with you as you leave. Everything can be replaced except YOU so it is important to leave as quickly as possible. Once you are out, call the Fire Service on 999 to report the fire.

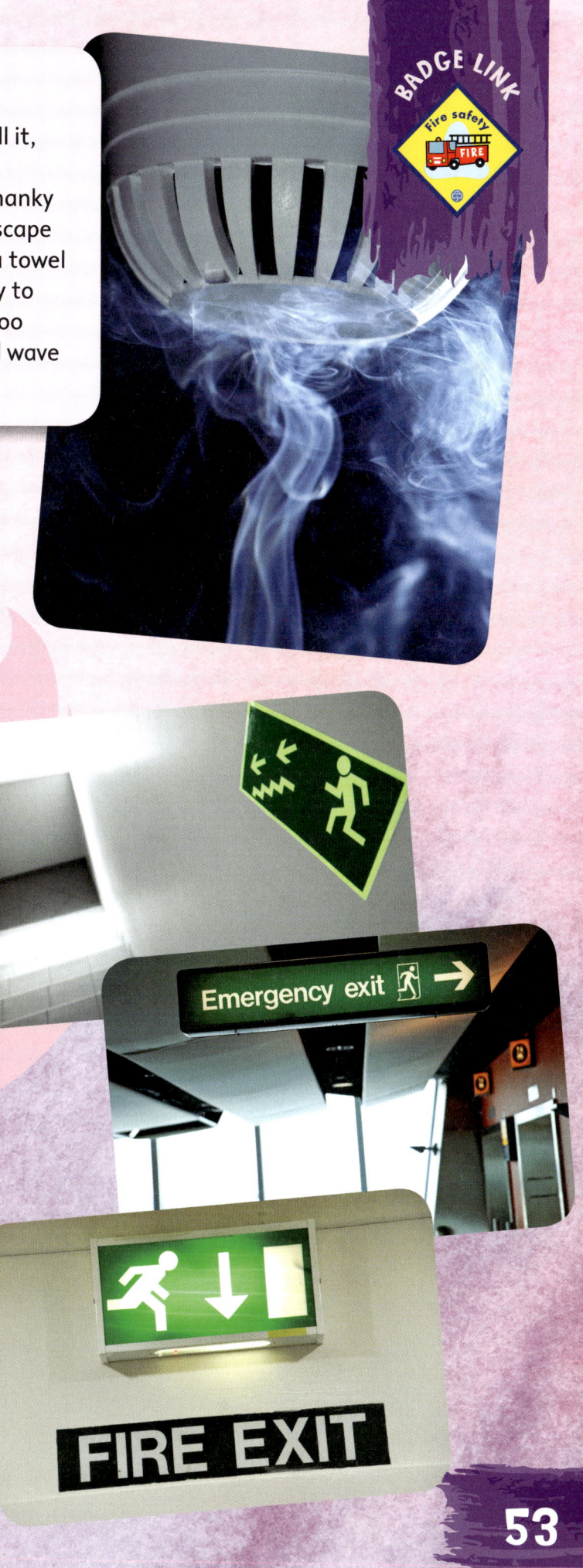

Strong teeth and a healthy heart

Caring for your teeth is easy and will give you something good to smile about.

Brush that plaque away!

Teeth need brushing twice a day – after breakfast and dinner. Brush gently, making little circles over the front, top and back of your teeth for three minutes. Don't forget to brush your tongue too. This will get rid of plaque, a white material that causes tooth decay and cavities (holes).

Sickly sweet is no treat

Did you know that fizzy and sugary drinks are very bad for teeth? They stick to the surface and encourage plaque to form. A tooth left in a glass of cola will dissolve in only a few days because the sugar and acid are so powerful. That's scary!

Make that appointment

Ask a parent or carer to book you an appointment to have your teeth checked every six months. A hygienist may clean all the places you find difficult to reach and your teeth will be so clean afterwards that they will sparkle. This is one appointment you just can't miss!

Illustrated by Nila Aye

Did you know your heart is a powerful muscle that pumps blood all over your body? Keep it healthy with these tips.

BADGE LINK

Healthy heart

Cook

You are what you eat
Eating the right foods is a great way to take care of your heart. Having five portions of fruit and veg each day will help you fight off colds and help your heart to pump blood. The fat in junk food makes your heart work much too hard and can lead to illness, so keep doughnuts, sweets and crisps for special occasions only.

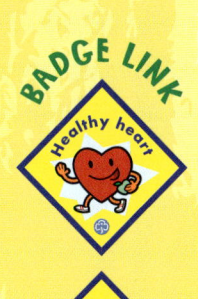

TAKE IT FURTHER:

Web safe

Visit the website www.bhf.org.uk/cbhf for games, articles and videos about treating your heart right.

Put out the fire
Smoking is very bad for your heart. The best way to protect your body is not to start. You'll be healthier and happier without cigarettes.

Get moving, get grooving
The more you move the better your heart will be. Find something you like to do and make some time each day to get moving. This can be dancing, using a skipping rope, swimming, climbing trees, walking your dog or playing tag. As your muscles get bigger your heart will get stronger.

55

Detective Brownie and the missing pets

This particular Monday was about as welcome as Scruff's weekly bath. I had a stack of unsolved cases piling up on my desk, all missing pets. I still had no clues.

Then Gran dropped by. Little Moopsie, her cat, had gone missing too. Actually Moopsie isn't little, she's the size of a baby elephant. Whoever took her would have needed a forklift truck. I told Gran I'd get her Moopsie back.

I headed out with Scruff. A hunch told me to head for the town farm to see Orwell the pig, the chief snout. No one could sniff out funny business (or food) better than Orwell.

'Morning, Detective B. I suppose you're here to ask about those missing pets?' Orwell snorted.

'Morning, Orwell. Smell anything unusual lately?' I asked.

'Methane,' he grunted. 'There's a lot about.'

'Methane? The greenhouse gas that helps keep the Earth warm? Hmm – thanks, Orwell.'

I headed over to Maisee-Lee, the farm cow. 'Morning, Maisee-Lee. Heard anything unusual lately?'

'Saucers,' she replied. 'The flying kind. I think we're being watched, Miss Detective!'

Methane? Flying saucers? Missing pets? I headed for Eddie the eagle. 'Morning, Eddie. Seen anything new lately?'

Eddie doesn't talk much. He looked at me, then at the sky. I followed his gaze up and saw something up there pretending to be the moon! That's when Scruff and I got abducted by an alien.

Next thing we knew we were inside a flying saucer. Our pilot was a three-eyed alien. 'Greetings, Detective Brownie and Dog. We would like to assist your investigation.'

'Sure,' I replied. 'Tell me what you know.'

It turned out the fake moon was a space station built by Earth scientists. The missing pets were all inside the space station. The scientists had been 'borrowing' them to harvest animal poo to turn into 'super methane'. (I know – GROSS!)

The aliens were going to close the space station down. They planned to erase the scientists' memories and replace them with information about how to take better care of Earth. The pets would be returned safely. Not the poo, though – I suggested they leave *that* in space.

Scruff and I were whizzed back to Earth with the pets. We returned them to their owners, including Moopsie. Case closed!

The scientists had discovered how to make super strong methane from animal poo, and they wanted to use it to heat up planet Mars!

Mars is colder than Earth because it's further away from the sun. Scientists think that if the Earth ever breaks down we might move to Mars if it's warm enough. The aliens weren't happy with that. It seems Mars already has people (well, alien people) living on it.

Quiz

How good are your powers of observation? Do they match up with Detective Brownie's? Test yourself with this quick quiz. No peeking back at the story for the answers! Check your answers on page 76.

1. What is Detective Brownie looking for?
2. What is the name of Gran's cat?
3. Who did Detective Brownie go to see first at the farm?
4. What did Maisee-Lee hear?
5. What is the eagle's name?
6. What is being turned to methane?
7. What is methane?
8. Why is Mars colder than Earth?

57

Mad about maths puzzles

You can find the answers on page 76.

1 Animal antics

Which creature is hiding in the grid? To find it, colour in the squares with these numbers in!

Colour in **RED** all squares with:
- an odd number
- a number that ends in 2
- a number smaller than 20.

Colour in **BLACK** all squares with:
- a number that ends in 0
- a number bigger than 100.

34	76	24	88	96	34	88	48	24	28
26	44	34	48	124	60	38	24	96	76
28		96	4	37	21	15	26		38
54	44	31	2	12	13	41	19	26	96
96	66	51	106	12	22	50	2	56	76
56	44	62	134	1	72	144	14	66	28
66	34	1	72	12	14	62	2	24	34
28		26	32	12	3	19	44		26
48	24	26	28	76	96	26	88	28	56
28	88	44	24	66	38	34	48	76	38

2 Number names

We have lots of ways of talking about numbers! Can you match up the words that mean the same thing?

A baker's dozen	Triple
Couple	Love (in tennis)
Nil (in football)	Pair
Hat-trick	Unlucky for some
Two little ducks	Two tens
Dozen	Ace
Score	22
Single	Number of months in the year

3. Pesky texts

You've just got a text message from your Sixer Emma. But it's come out scrambled! Can you work out the message?

- 2: abc
- 3: def
- 4: ghi
- 5: jkl
- 6: mno
- 7: pqrs
- 8: tuv
- 9: wxyz

7773363362233777 99966688777 7777944466444664 2226667777888633 6633998 9333355. 77773333 99966688 28 84433 7666666555!

4. Lost in numbers

See if you can follow the hidden path from beginning to end.

Start on the blue square marked 4 and follow the directions below.

Each time you land on a square, move that number of spaces.

If a square is **blue**, move north.

If it's **yellow**, move east.

If you land on a **green** square, move south.

And if it's **red**, move west.

Which exit do you get to?

Party food!

WHAT TO DO

INGREDIENTS

- 50g chopped walnuts
- 2tbsp chopped dried sour cherries or cranberries
- 2tbsp runny honey
- a pinch of salt and pepper
- 1 baguette, sliced
- 250g ricotta cheese
- 1tbsp chopped mint leaves

Tasty tartines

This recipe makes a small plate of open sandwiches. Be sure to make enough for everyone to enjoy.

1 Stir the walnuts, dried fruit, honey, salt and pepper together in a bowl.

2 Toast the bread and then spread the slices with the ricotta cheese.

3 Spoon the honey mixture over the cheese and sprinkle the mint on top.

TAKE IT FURTHER

For extra flavour, ask an adult to help you toast the walnuts in a pan for a few minutes before starting the recipe – but be careful not to let them burn.

WHAT TO DO

Cheesy pitta crisps

These crisps can be eaten with hummus, salsa or other dips, or just as they are. This recipe makes a party-size bowlful.

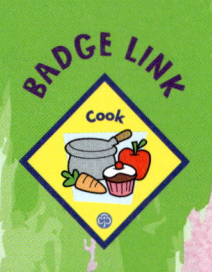

BADGE LINK — Cook

1 Preheat the oven to 180°c or gas mark 3. Cut each pitta bread in half horizontally so you have 2 large ovals. Cut each oval into 6 pieces.

Be safe

INGREDIENTS

- 6 pitta breads
- 6tbsp olive oil
- 70g parmesan cheese, grated
- a pinch of salt and black pepper

2 Brush each piece with oil and sprinkle with cheese and salt and pepper. Arrange the pieces in a single layer on two baking sheets.

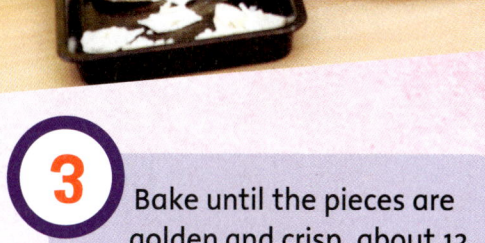

3 Bake until the pieces are golden and crisp, about 12 minutes. Cool on a wire rack.

Surprising facts

How many of these facts are new to you? Do you think Brownies have changed a lot over the years? Are you surprised at some of the things Brownies have got up to?

Brownies were originally called Rosebuds in 1914. But the image of a rosebud did not seem to fit girls full of energy and mischief so in 1915 the name was changed to Brownies.

Would you prefer to be a Rosebud?

Brownies used to have a grand salute with which they greeted visitors to their meetings or at Brownie revels. The Brownies would crouch down on the floor then jump up, saying: 'Tu-whit-tu-who-oo-oo-oo!' three times like an owl.

Do you know any bird calls? Can you think up a salute of your own?

As part of the Brownie section's 21st birthday, Brownies had a 'Lend a Hand' week when they tried to do as many Good Turns for their friends and family as they could.

That's a lot of helping hands!

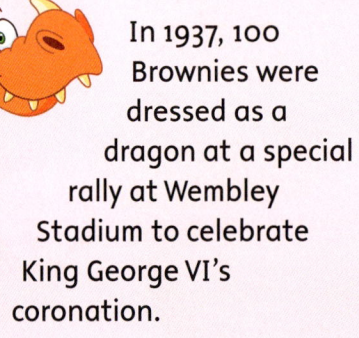

In 1937, 100 Brownies were dressed as a dragon at a special rally at Wembley Stadium to celebrate King George VI's coronation.

Roar!

During the Second World War many Brownie units had to meet on Saturday afternoons or only received letters from their Brownie Leaders instead of having meetings. Blackouts and bombing stopped many Brownies going to meetings.

How would we stay in touch today?

about Brownies

During the Second World War Brownies helped the war effort by collecting clothes, waste paper and acorns, picking fruit, gathering firewood and running errands.

What could you do to help others today?

In 1948 a film called *Brownie Days* was produced to show what it was like to be a Brownie.

How many things do you think have changed since then? What would you film?

A 'tea-making fortnight' was organised for the Brownies' 70th birthday. Each Brownie was challenged to make 30 cups of tea for members of the public.

Do you know how to make a cup of tea? How about 30 of them?

A Brownie Exhibition Week was held in 1951 to promote Brownies. Displays were held in shop windows to show Brownie activities and holidays.

Have you ever seen the front window displays at the Girlguiding UK office in London?

Until 1968 a Brownie had to be eight years old before she could go on a sleepover or Brownie Holiday.

Have you had your first sleepover or Brownie Holiday yet? Where was it?

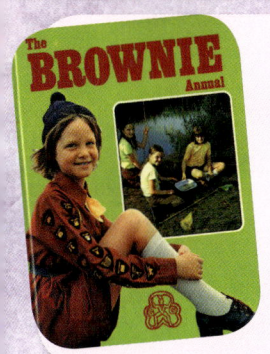

The first *Brownie Annual* was published in 1958.

Can you figure out how many annuals have been published since then?

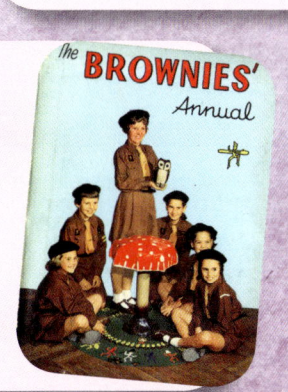

In 2001, 380 Brownies had a sleepover in the Science Museum in London.

That's a lot of whispering after lights-out!

In 1970 a Brownie unit from Oban was chosen to carry the Queen's Message to the Commonwealth Games in Edinburgh. They had to leave Oban at 5:45am to do this.

Do you know where Oban is? How would you get to Edinburgh from there?

Mexican hot chocolate party

Did you know that drinking chocolate was enjoyed in Mexico over 3,000 years ago? Why not celebrate a birthday or special occasion with a Mexican-themed chocolate tea party? Or have one at a Brownie meeting! You can start with the decorations…

YOU WILL NEED

- a foil roasting dish or baking tray
- a permanent marker
- scissors
- a hole punch
- an old table mat or piece of cardboard
- toothpicks
- ribbon

WHAT TO DO

Tin trinket decorations

Making ornaments out of tin is a traditional art form in Mexico. Tinsmiths use lots of different tools to punch holes and make patterns. Have a go yourself!

1 Draw a shape on the base of the metal dish with the permanent marker and cut it out.

2 Make a hole at the top of the shape so that you can hang it up.

3 Place the shape over the old table mat or cardboard. Using the toothpick, lightly make a pattern of dents in your shape. Be careful not to push too hard and make holes in the metal.

4 When you have finished your pattern, thread some ribbon through the hole at the top and hang up your decoration.

Hot chocolate hints

You've got hot chocolate powder in your mug and have warmed up some milk – but what comes next? Try out these ideas for giving your hot chocolate a special twist.

BADGE LINK
Cook
Craft

Orange zest
Take a piece of orange peel and hit it with a spoon or rolling pin. Then pop it into your hot chocolate (but don't eat it).

Vanilla
Stir ¼ tsp of vanilla extract into your hot chocolate.

Peanut butter
Add a dessertspoon of smooth peanut butter and stir until it melts.

Coconut milk
Instead of adding hot milk, try adding coconut milk.

Ice cream
Drop a small scoop of ice cream in your drink to make it super creamy.

Raspberry jam
Stir a dessertspoon of seedless raspberry jam into your hot chocolate.

Competition

How would you like to win an amazing prize pack? Tell us more about how much fun it is to be a Brownie.

Prize pack:
* The Brownie Cookbook
* apron
* melamine tray
* resin cooking bear
* sling bag

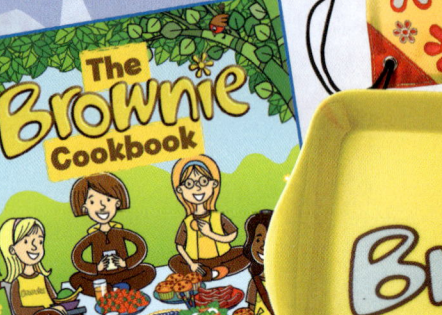

Competition rules:
Make a list of five new things you'd like to do at Brownies and ten things you already love to do.

Send your entry to:
Brownie Annual 2013 Competition, Girlguiding UK, 17–19 Buckingham Palace Road, London SW1W 0PT. The closing date for the competition is **25 February 2013**.

Brownie shopping

Photo clip
8353 £6

Clip purse
2041 £3.95

Mug
2388 £2.75

Monkey clip
7116 £3.50

Backpack
8701 £10

Watch
8376 £9

Bookmarks
8377 £2.20

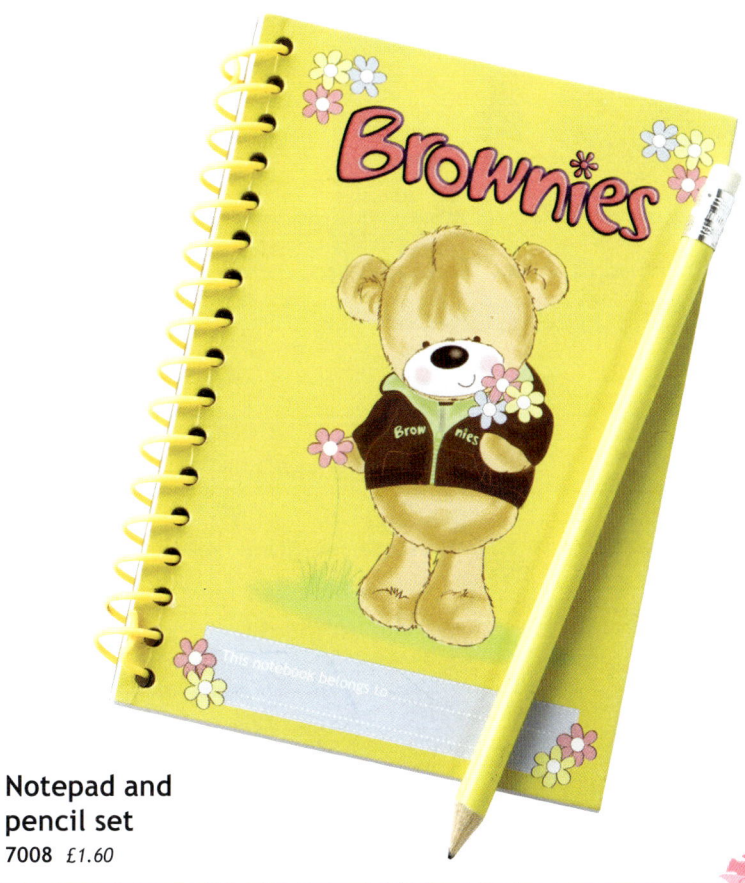

Notepad and pencil set
7008 £1.60

📱 **0161 941 2237**
to find your nearest volunteer shop or to order from the catalogue,
or visit www.girlguidingukshop.co.uk

67

The power of air!

WHAT TO DO

Activity 1

Hovercraft can travel across land, water and mud because they actually float on a cushion of air! Using air like this creates less friction – the force that slows moving things down. Hovercraft are used to cross rivers and rescue people at sea. They even have races!

YOU WILL NEED

- the lid from a sports drink bottle that you can click open and closed
- strong glue
- an old CD or DVD you don't want any more
- a balloon

1 With an adult's help, glue the bottle lid over the hole in the middle of the CD and leave to dry.

2 Open the bottle cap and stretch the neck of the balloon over the cap.

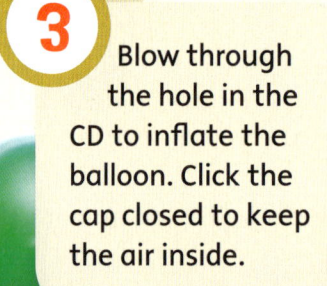

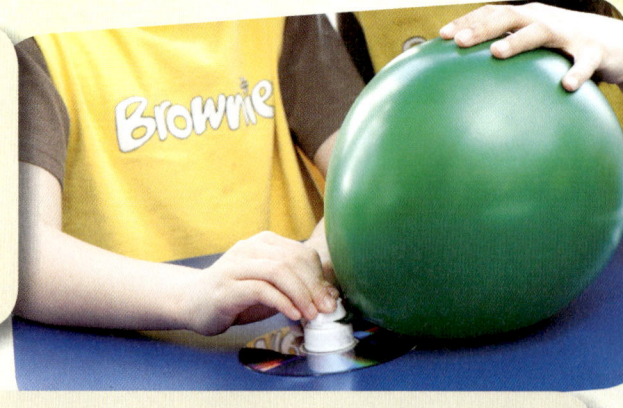

3 Blow through the hole in the CD to inflate the balloon. Click the cap closed to keep the air inside.

4 Place your hovercraft on a smooth flat surface like a table or tiled floor and open the cap. The air escaping from the balloon is forced under the CD and makes a cushion of air for it to float on!

WHAT TO DO

Activity 2

You can also use the power of air to protect things as they fall. Parachutes trap air inside them so the passenger falls slowly to the ground.

1 Cut out square parachutes from different materials. Cut a hole the size of a 5p coin in the centre of each.

2 Tie a piece of string to each corner of your parachute and attach them to the passengers.

3 Drop the parachutes from the same height each time – like a chair or the top of some stairs – and time how long it takes each one to reach the ground. Make a note of each time and see which material made the best parachute!

YOU WILL NEED

- materials for parachutes such as plastic carrier bags, newspaper or kitchen roll
- string
- something light and unbreakable like small plastic animals
- a stopwatch

BADGE LINK — Science investigator

What material was the parachute made of?	How many seconds did it take to reach the ground?

Dot Com Brownie to the rescue

It all started at school. Evie's friends were all talking about Teenzone, a new website that people could use to talk to each other and share pictures and music. It sounded really exciting and Evie wanted to join her school and Brownie friends on the website.

Aaliyah went to Evie's house after Brownies. 'Let's join Teenzone,' Aaliyah said. 'I know how.'

Evie borrowed her mother's laptop. She knew she should ask to use it but her mother might have lots of questions about Teenzone. Evie wanted to be a member like Aaliyah. Evie chose the username 'Eviebelle2004'. She entered her date of birth and a password, and clicked 'Create Account'.

A big red message box popped up on the screen saying: 'You must be at least 13 years old to create an account on Teenzone.'

Evie looked at Aaliyah and said 'I can't create an account on Teenzone. I'm not old enough.' Aaliyah told Evie not to worry about the message because all of her friends on Teenzone had ignored it when they signed up.

Illustrated by Lorraine O'Connell

Evie wasn't sure what to do. She knew that she shouldn't break the rules but all of her friends were on Teenzone, and she really wanted to join them. Evie decided to lie about her age and go on to create her profile.

When the time came for Aaliyah to go home, she told Evie that she would sign in to Teenzone later that evening so that they could chat. She said that her name on Teenzone was Aaliyah123. Aaliyah left and Evie put her mother's laptop away and began to do her homework.

Later that evening Evie visited the Teenzone website. A message flashed up when she logged in: 'Aaliyah123 wants to be your friend. Please click here to accept her request.' Evie accepted the request and began chatting to Aaliyah.

They spoke about how much fun Teenzone was and how difficult their maths homework was.

Aaliyah told Evie about all the new friends that she had met on Teenzone. She suggested that Evie should become friends with them as well so they could chat.

Evie didn't know who any of Aaliyah's new friends were and she told Aaliyah, 'I don't think I should make them my friends on Teenzone if I don't know them in real life.'

'That's fine,' Aaliyah replied, 'but Teenzone is more fun if you become friends with lots of people even if you've never met them. Imagine having hundreds of friends!'

Just then, Evie's father called to her, 'Dinner's ready, come on Evie.'

Evie told Aaliyah that she had to leave the computer and have dinner. Aaliyah said, 'Okay, I'm going to stay on for a bit longer and meet some new people. I'll see you in school tomorrow.'

Evie woke up early the next day. She couldn't wait to get in to school to talk to Aaliyah about Teenzone. But there was no sign of Aaliyah at school that day, and Evie was worried that she might be sick.

Evie went to Aaliyah's house after school. When she went up to Aaliyah's room, Evie could see that her friend had been crying. 'What's wrong, Aaliyah?' she asked.

Aaliyah turned on her computer to show Evie her Teenzone profile. Aaliyah had added a photograph to her profile and some of her Teenzone friends had said some really mean things. They had called her names like Stink-face.

Evie didn't know what to say. Suddenly the Teenzone website disappeared from the computer screen and in its place was a picture of a girl. She waved at the girls and then

71

to their amazement, she climbed right out of the computer screen and sat beside them on the bed.

'Hi! I'm Dot Com Brownie,' she said.

Aaliyah and Evie stared at Dot Com Brownie. She had long red hair tied up in bunches and wore a Brownie T-shirt and trousers with pink glittery trainers.

She smiled at the girls and announced, 'I'm here because I think you're having some trouble online.'

'Yes,' replied Aaliyah, 'my new friends on Teenzone have been really mean to me. They've been calling me names and saying terrible things. I don't know what to do.'

Dot Com Brownie explained, 'They were bullying you. Bullying online is called cyber-bullying and it is just as serious as bullying in school.'

Aaliyah thought for a moment and then said, 'If it's just like bullying in school, I should tell my parents or teachers. And I probably shouldn't have accepted requests to be friends from people I don't know.'

Dot Com Brownie smiled. 'That's right, your parents or teacher will be able to give you advice. And you should never accept friend requests online from people you don't know. Now, is there something else you should have done or not done?'

Aaliyah had forgotten, but Evie remembered. 'When we signed up to Teenzone we lied about our age. We only did it because our friends said that it was really good fun. Now I know that we shouldn't have done that.'

'I think my work here is done,' Dot Com Brownie said. She stood up and dived head-first back in to the computer screen. When Aaliyah and Evie looked at the screen again the Teenzone website had reappeared.

Aaliyah ran downstairs and asked her mother for help. Her mother came up and saw what had happened. She and Aaliyah deleted the profile on Teenzone. Aaliyah apologised to her mother for not telling her about the website.

Evie went home that evening and told her father everything that had happened. He helped her to delete her Teenzone profile, and told her to talk to him if she ever wanted to set up a profile on a website like Teenzone in the future.

Follow the rules below to help to keep you safe on any website

1. Don't post information that could help someone to find you – for example, photos, your address, your phone number or your last name.
2. Don't post photos of yourself online as anyone could download them or share them with anyone else.
3. Don't break the rules of the websites that you use. Many of these rules are there to protect you and other people using the website.
4. Don't forget that people can lie about who they are online.
5. Don't meet up with anyone you have been chatting to and don't know in real life.
6. Don't give your passwords to anyone or they could pretend to be you online.
7. Don't forget to tell parents, carers, a teacher or Brownie Leader if something happens online that worries or upsets you.

With thanks to the Girl Scouts of the USA and Minimentors for the ideas contained within these guidelines.

Web safe

Word puzzles

How many of these brain busters can you solve in one go? You might have to come back to some of them! Turn to page 77 for the answers.

Activity word search

B	S	Q	K	A	R	A	O	K	E	F	G
O	F	A	H	E	A	T	G	E	N	N	R
I	E	U	R	S	F	N	X	K	I	M	A
G	N	K	T	C	T	E	H	R	L	O	S
R	C	D	D	A	H	Y	E	F	O	E	S
Z	I	P	W	I	R	E	Y	C	P	K	S
T	N	I	U	R	T	V	R	G	M	I	L
E	G	F	O	N	S	I	T	Y	A	Z	E
R	E	F	E	O	N	A	C	S	R	L	D
G	N	I	B	M	I	L	C	U	T	B	G
P	R	H	I	G	H	R	O	P	E	S	E
O	S	E	L	B	A	T	A	L	F	N	I

There are loads of exciting activities for you to try at the Training and Activity Centres. Find as many of these words as you can and tick off all the ones you have done before. Which one would you like to try next?

- ☐ Archery
- ☐ Canoe
- ☐ Climbing
- ☐ Fencing
- ☐ Grass sledge
- ☐ High ropes
- ☐ Inflatables
- ☐ Karaoke
- ☐ Orienteering
- ☐ Raft
- ☐ Trampoline
- ☐ Zipwire

Crossword scrambler

All the words below are things you might need on a Brownie adventure. Can you fit them all into the grid? Do you know which activities they are used for?

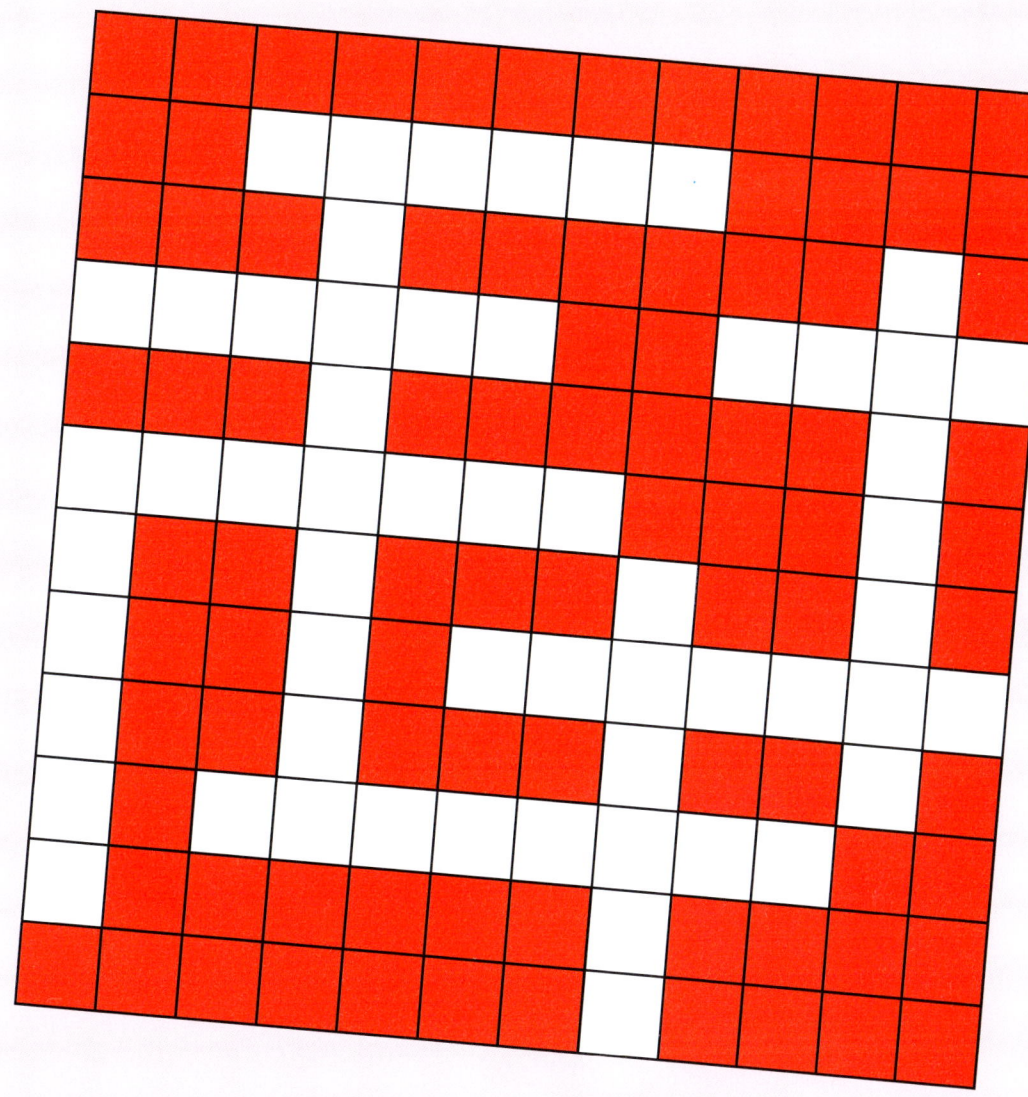

FOIL   QUIVER   HELMET
ARROWS   PADDLE   DIABOLO
BARRELS   HARNESS   TEAMWORK   ADVENTURE

Riddles

1. In what sport do the losers go forwards and the winners go backwards?
2. What happens once in a minute, twice in a moment but never in a century?
3. What gets whiter the dirtier it gets?
4. The girls in Jennie's Six are called April, May, June, July, August and…?
5. What word becomes shorter when you add letters to it?

Answers

Pages 26-27 – Jolly jokes and baffling brain-teasers

a) Your word
b) The bark of a tree
c) Zero
d) Silence
e) A smile

Pages 40-41 – The big Brownie quiz

1. c
2. true
3. b
4. a
5. c
6. a
7. c
8. b
9. a (The Queen was a Guide)
10. true

Pages 57 – Detective Brownie and the missing pets

1. Pets
2. Little Moopsie
3. Orwell
4. Flying Saucers
5. Eddie
6. Animal poo
7. A gas
8. It's further away from the sun

Pages 58-59 Mad about maths puzzles

Animal antics

34	76	24	88	96	34	88	48	24	28
26	44	34	48			38	24	96	76
28		96					26		38
54	44						26		96
96	66						56		76
56	44						66		28
62	34							24	34
28		26					44		26
48	24	26	28	76	96	26	88	28	56
28	88	44	24	66	38	34	48	76	38

Number names

A baker's dozen	Unlucky for some
Couple	Pair
Nil (in football)	Love (in tennis)
Hat-trick	Triple
Two little ducks	22
Dozen	Number of months in the year
Score	Two tens
Single	Ace

Pesky texts

Remember your swimming costume next week. See you at the pool!

Lost in numbers

You will finish at Exit B.

76

Pages 74-75 - Word puzzles

Activity word search

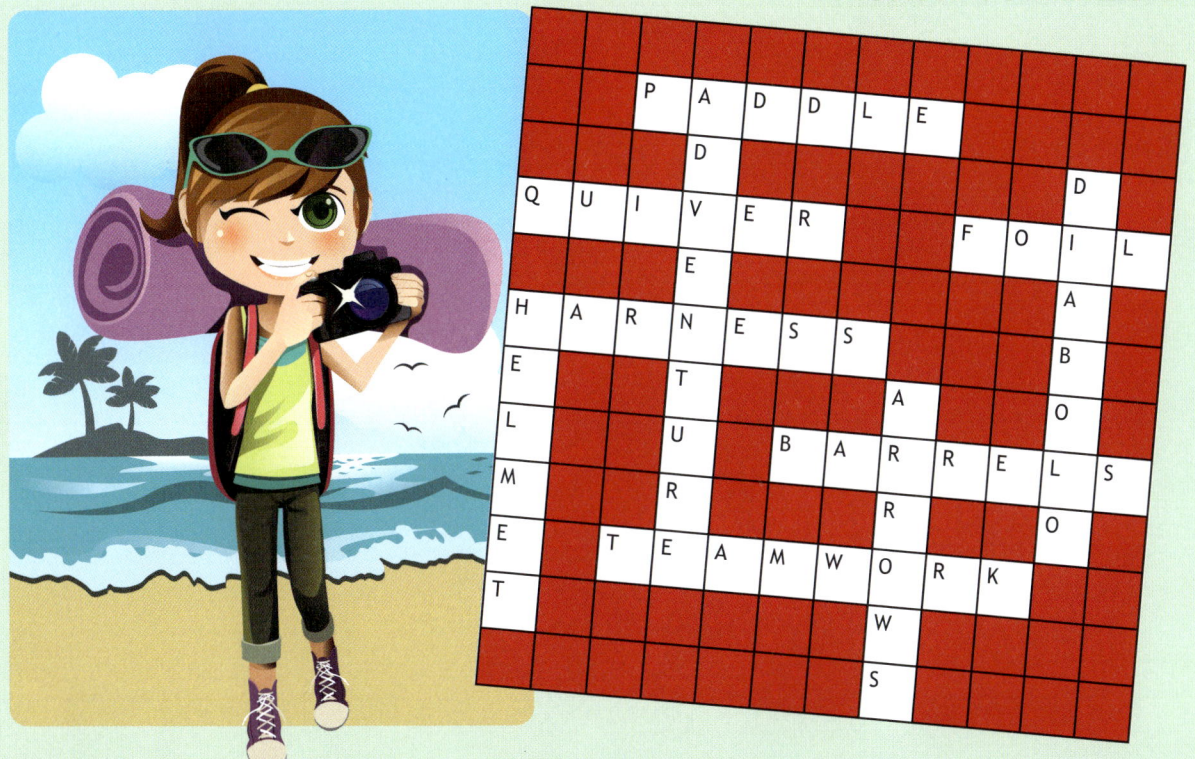

Crossword scrambler

Riddles

1. Tug of war   2. The letter 'm'   3. A blackboard   4. Jennie   5. Short

World of adventure

How many activities can you count in this picture?

Illustrated by Nila Aye